Quartet

Also by Angela Ball:

Possession
Kneeling Between Parked Cars
Recombinant Lives

Quartet

Angela Ball

Carnegie Mellon University Press
Pittsburgh 1995

ACKNOWLEDGMENTS

The author and publisher make grateful acknowledgment to the editors of the following publications for permission to reprint these poems:

The Cream City Review: "Nora," Parts 1 & 3.
The Malahat Review: "Nancy Cunard."
Negative Capability: "Sylvia Beach."
The Southern Review: "Jean Rhys," Parts 1, 3, & 5.

Acknowledgments are also due the following authors, whose works informed the poems:

Noel Riley Fitch. *Sylvia Beach and the Lost Generation.* (New York: W.W. Norton and Company, 1983).
Brenda Maddox. *Nora: A Biography of Nora Joyce.* (New York: Fawcett Columbine, 1988).
Padraic O Laoi. *Nora Barnacle Joyce: A Portrait.* (Galway: Kennys Bookshops and Art Galleries Ltd., 1982).
Anne Chisholm. *Nancy Cunard: A Biography.* (New York: Alfred A. Knopf, 1979).
Hugh Ford, Editor. *Nancy Cunard: Brave Poet, Indomitable Rebel.* (Philadelphia: Chilton Book Company, 1968).
Carole Angier. *Jean Rhys: Life and Work.* (Boston: Little, Brown and Company, 1990).
David Plante. *Difficult Women: A memoir of three: Sonia Orwell, Jean Rhys, Germaine Greer.* (New York: Atheneum, 1983).
Thomas F. Staley. *Jean Rhys: A Critical Study.* (Austin: University of Texas Press, 1979).
Francis Wyndham and Dianna Melly, Editors. *Jean Rhys: Letters 1931-66.* (London: Penguin Books, 1985).

These poems were written with the support of the Mississippi Arts Council and the National Endowment for the Arts.

The publication of this book is supported by grants from the National Endowment for the Arts in Washington D.C., a Federal agency, and from the Pennsylvania Council on the Arts.

Library of Congress Catalog Card Number 94-70464
ISBN 0-88748-188-4
ISBN 0-88748-189-2 Pbk

Printed and bound in the United States of America

10 9 8 7 6 5 4 3 2 1

CONTENTS

for Kim

for Noel Riley Fitch, author of *Sylvia Beach and the Lost Generation*

SYLVIA BEACH (1887-1962)

Sylvia Beach was born in Baltimore, Maryland, to Eleanor Orbison and the Reverend Sylvester Beach. Sylvia first spent time in Paris as a young girl, while her father served as a pastor at the American church. Sylvia loved France and the French, and soon decided to settle in Paris. One day in 1917 she entered Adrienne Monnier's bookshop, and the two struck up a friendship that would become life-long love. Adrienne led Sylvia to her vocation: Shakespeare and Company Bookshop, which opened on 17 November 1919. It quickly became the literary center of English speaking Paris—serving not only as bookstore and lending library, but as bank, post office, and sanctuary for the likes of Ernest Hemingway, F. Scott Fitzgerald, Ezra Pound, T.S. Eliot, and countless other expatriates. Most of all, Sylvia and Shakespeare and Company were all things to one person: James Joyce, who found in Sylvia a friend, a loyal supporter of his work, and—when censorship threatened to keep *Ulysses* from seeing daylight—a publisher. The publication of *Ulysses* was fraught with financial, logistical, and legal difficulties, but Sylvia was more than a match for them all.

1

Sylvia Beach, American
Aged 54.
Has no Horse.

I never understood why that notation
beside my name. Every week of the occupation
I signed in. The thin book of Americans
was always getting lost—I found it
for the commissaire.

From about this time I decided
to own my age. Always before
I was younger by 9 years.

Shakespeare and Company, bookshop,
held its breath
between two wars. How much
happened? For one thing
a day at the sea, at Hyères.
My ridiculous facsimile
of a dive. Gide shrugging:
Pas fameux! While all the time,
buoyed by a life belt, Adrienne
floated calmly near shore. Joyce,
impatient in Paris: When's Beach
coming back?

I'm alone, already in future.

Wind scans the backs of leaves.

Once, at the Foire D'Orsay with friends
Larbaud, Fargue, Marie,
and Adrienne, a carnival picture
put us in one boat. I'm still in there.

I can't doubt S. Beach, publisher—
I still dream I have to arrange

the printing. I travel on foot
carrying the ms. in brown paper,
the whole time about to be struck
by lightning, *Ulysses* burned. Sometimes
it flies apart and I run after, over mountain ranges
one way, through desert another.

I left home lightly, sure
not to make much
of any love. Settled on a woman,
a bookshop, and a man.

I went to Spire's party.
There, drooping in a corner,
was James Joyce.

One noticed his hands. They were narrow,
with heavy rings on the middle and third fingers
of the left.

What do you do? he asked, then held a small black book
close to his eyes to write Shakespeare and Co.
and the address.

2

Something else definite
for the ledger:
Adrienne Monnier, owner
of La Libraire A. Monnier,
was my friend
37 years.

I called myself "business man."

Adrienne and I spent holidays in the mountains
with the Monniers, at Les Déserts.
Our bedroom was a corner
of the hayloft—strings stretched across
to hang our clothes, a chicken crate

(complete with chickens) our table.
One night at three a.m. we looked down through the boards
to watch a calf being born
by lantern light, with everyone present.
At daybreak the stable doors opened,
and out poured the cattle like a crowd
leaving the theatre.

Adrienne loved me first. I was glad.
Never let a man
touch you, Mother said.
I could never disobey.

Everyone, Twain said, is a moon
with a dark side.

3

The American exiles had an air
of having become their own creations.
Of variable interest.

George Antheil, composer, took the room upstairs.
He regularly lost his key, and climbed heroically in
over the balcony.

The first afternoon I met Hemingway,
he drew up his trouser leg
to acquaint me with his wounds.

I was Jack Sprat
to all their extravagance.
They needed me for contrast.
Frugal, modest, clean.

Ezra the P.T. Barnum of poetry.
Antheil determined to match the world's commotion
in music. Gertrude announcing
to Samuel Putnam:
American Literature *is* Gertrude Stein.

Oh egos whose very size
baffles all criticism!

Star-struck McAlmon could have stuck.
The trouble was, his ideas dwarfed
the execution. He'd rather talk.

Joyce, Irish, and perhaps
because of that a martyr
to martyrdom
and damn proud.

Sylvia a good bookseller?
I praised first editions so well
I convinced myself to keep them.

What I did was save words
and secrets.

4

Joyce and I read *Ulysses*
together, when he was writing it.
He looked broken up
as he sat, as if the parts
had wandered in from separate places.

He was frightened of all dogs—
I had to shoo my little white one
out the back way when I saw him coming.

Frightened also of thunder. And two nuns
walking together. But black cats
were good.

He was exacting. Wanted the precise Aegean blue
to wrap *Ulysses*. It *was* the true color.

I thought George Bernard Shaw would subscribe,
so made a bet with Joyce: Voltigeur cigars
against a silk handkerchief. The letter came:
"I should like to put a cordon around Dublin;
round up every male person
between 15 and 30; force them to read all that
foul mouthed, foul minded
derision and obscenity."

There's more—something about a "young barbarian"
(read as S. Beach) "beglamoured by the excitements
and enthusiasms that art stirs
in passionate material." For days
I dreamed of big beards, campfires, knives,
passion. It didn't fit.

5

Miss Weaver hoped that all her money
would feed genius. Genius was hungry!
Even when she found out how much Joyce spent
on dinners and tips, she gave.

She didn't need to see Joyce,
know him. Just help.
That wasn't easy. *Ulysses* was declared obscene
in London, and the copies I sent Miss Weaver
confiscated and burned.
How little of us escapes
the King's chimney!

6

Nora mattered. Lucia.
Georgio, sometimes. Others he took
as his due, luck.

Our needs crossed—his
for mother, to be cared

for, mine—
He loved lush women. Plump Adrienne
would have stood a better chance!

Adrienne—I wouldn't say
I gave myself over—wasted.
The gift was itself
prize. The having given.

Ended when Padraic Colum—one of my successors
with Joyce—came to talk about rights.
He had the face of a person
who has come to speak about money.
"You're standing in his way,"
he said. So finished.

I now think *he* didn't know.
Paul Leon was with him then, too—
Paul did his best,
along with following his own love.
New friends have to seem improvements.
And seeing was Joyce's strength never.

I know now
calculation belongs to the lover
not the beloved.

After Joyce died, I talked to Paul—
we two lost in a trap
looked around and discussed
what life used to be like.

There's a day even regret
is lost.

Soon after, Paul was arrested
and executed for being a Jew.

Also Françoise, my helper, was taken
to Auschwitz, where she died.

When I went to the Gestapo to beg for her,
they said I had a black mark on my name
because of my friends.

Comes a day when there's no pity—
not even the need.
When no one's left how mourn?
Sympathy begins at home
and so it ends.

Age immured in age,
and dust of moth wings,
water flowing on water.

A fainter moment
you couldn't find.
War denatures,
and loss.

"Why say very beautiful," I heard Joyce say
the day I met him. "Beautiful is enough."

7

Joyce was always trying
to get me reading Yeats.
I like French poets—Valéry—
best. But I caught
a line: . . . *though they don't say it in school*
a woman must labour
to be beautiful.

I never needed compliments—
those who treated me as a special genius
because of my sex
also thought I was pretending,
that I somehow operated on a string
of passing impulses
that must one day *kaput.*

The Nazis did away with the store.
One day an officer wanted my signed copy
of *Finnegans Wake*. I sold him Gorman's biography
instead. He returned two weeks later,
still asking for *Finnegans Wake*.
"We're coming to confiscate all your goods
today." "All right," I said.

A friend and I went to work,
moved everything to the third floor—
all the books and photographs,
the furniture. I had a carpenter
dismantle the shelves. Within two hours
not a single thing was left.
A house painter had painted out the name, Shakespeare
and Company, on the front of 12 rue de l'Odeon.
The date was 1941.

One day Hemingway came to liberate the shop—
grabbed me and spun me around
while everyone in the street chanted, "Sylvia!"

I never re-opened.
I said one should not attempt anything
twice.

8

My mother died in 1927
while visiting me—from a heart condition
and shame at being arrested
for an old, mistaken charge
of shoplifting. I told no one
about the overdose she took.

My father died.
Joyce died in a hospital,
three a.m., alone.

I envied Hemingway his wounds—
plumage to be adored. Women's troubles
are internal, said Emily Dickinson, "Where
the meanings are."

I came back from a visit to America
to find our friend Gisèle
living with Adrienne.

Adrienne was ill. Her ears held crumbling
land, cries of souls, wingflaps,
torrents, banshee screech
of a thousand window frames
wrenched open.
"I am going to death without fear," she wrote,
"knowing that I found a mother on being born
here and that I shall likewise find a mother
in the other life."

She took an overdose of sleeping tablets, died.

She knew everything, Adrienne.

I see no remedy
for the swooping down of death
on one you love.

9

Paris, a star's stretched points.
Dove gray, pearl gray. One flying leaf
resembling a feather escaped
from a lady's elaborate hat.

Streets cant and jackknife
to invite. Joyce said, "Paris
is like myself. A haughty ruin
or a decayed reveller."

Paris is old, and knows. The Seine
in its dungeon of banks,
its one age.

❖NORA

for Brenda Maddox, author of *Nora: A Biography of Nora Joyce*

NORA BARNACLE JOYCE (1884-1951)

Nora Barnacle was born in Galway, in Ireland. Her mother was Annie Healy, a seamstress and dressmaker; her father was Tom Barnacle, an itinerant baker. In 1904 she left Galway for Dublin, to work as a domestic at Finn's Hotel. Walking up Nassau Street on June 10, 1904, she met James Joyce. In defiance of convention—and her own hopes of marriage and traditional home life—she ran away with Joyce to the continent, and lived with him in Trieste, Paris, and Zurich until his death in 1941. She sustained him and his work in ways impossible to estimate. The prototype and inspiration for Molly Bloom in *Ulysses*, for Joyce Nora was the woman of all women.

1

I was doorkeeper at the convent,
stayed just inside the gate,
between silence and the noisy smells
of the fishmarket, the stables,
peatsmoke, cabbages and potatoes
elbowing each other in cauldrons.

I ran away to Dublin
only to catch myself
in the dusty travelling case
of Finn's Hotel. The iron beds
breathed chill, the walls sponged rain
and went to muttering.

My name made one more X
in the streets' ledger.
The breeze begging something green—
the last thing it needed,
another skirt to tug.

I'd thought by that time
to have worn my wedding clothes
for a photograph—to have been
one of those girls sitting very straight
as if marriage were a brace.

Instead I had the puddles'
thousand gray cameos—a cloud a strip of lace
crossing the sky.
In Galway they'd say,
Better crab apples than air. Go back?
I'd rather roll down a hillside of briars.

Life was all legs moving place to place,
getting and carrying. Fields or waves or sheets
to bend above. Snuffed candle flame's
soot scrawl.

Cleaning a room, I stopped to peer
through the window at a horse,
his back steaming, standing with one cocked leg,
the driver's pipe smoke blowing sideways.
I waved at him, though he wouldn't see me.

I stripped a licorice-striped pillow,
gaunt prisoner who lets out a wheeze
and a brown feather.

Where does all the dust
come from? Comes not like an olive twig
in a dove's beak, no triumph in it.
Dust is as it does.
We send it back to water
to rub a stone.

2

How morning light levers the big tree!
Orange-gold with black tatters,
dark branches travelling through.

I was born, I heard, in the workhouse hospital,
famous for the size and strength of its door—
to get in, one had to lean on it
one's full weight.

Things in their time stand amazed,
the sun's self in a leaf gap
shoots pins of every color, a cockade.

We girls went dancing at the crossroads,
whirled faster than our heads could follow.
I strolled with Michael Feeney at Salthill.
The wind made us whisper close, sent the waves
running to catch themselves.

He gave me this bracelet. Then he was sick,
and I couldn't see him.

In Rahoon cemetery my heart's halved.
He's in the gateless place, who would have been my life
in Galway, our children. I was and am that Nora Feeney.

Mulvagh I walked with at Nun's Island, past the huge
jail walls. He was Protestant—and Uncle Tommy found that
fine excuse to beat me, though I begged on my knees.

When I left for Dublin I said goodbye to no one—
not Mulvagh, not my mother.

3

I think of a spinster, her pulse
tap tapping in a cave, whose dreams
haul a baby in from the river.
It laughs, tickled by salmon.

The unseen baby dreams against her
all her life, like a bicycle against a wall.
She hopes her death will be sweet,
so people come to smooth her hands
and look gently at her face
and not fear her.

The bay swerves and wheels on its pins,
the grass lies in its lazy bed
with kneaded clods and holes
the badger makes. When people have talked
all their talk, rain begins,
dragged forward by branches.

Before I can remember, my mother
gave me to my grandmother, to make room.
When I was in my box bed, a cricket
sang very loudly. Wagon wheels cracked
against stones.

When Grandmother died I lived with Uncle
and his rules. My father lived away.
He was a journeyman baker wherever they needed
extra bread. Jim said he drank his buns and loaves
like a man. He should talk!

I arrived in Dublin in a winter
of rain and snow. City fish
coursed the Liffey's old come-along
go-along. The city disputing, asking,
haggling with all its lungs.

Winter afternoons at Finn's the bar light
like smudged drawing paper
sketched with shadows, beards
fit to be scrub brushes. Shoulders
held up by shadows.

Meat stewed on the bone for them
in the ovens their thin wives
warm their toes under.

Down the fine street,
the gray mein of rich houses,
softness peeked from within,
a nod of pink petals.

At home they said, That Nora—
Dublin's got her
by the thin edge of the wedge.

I woke to frost's madness
on my window. Snow's strangeness
and comfort lit in the sheets,
no trace of before,
no hint of after.

How tired must the ground be
under the hotel—such heaviness
of marriage and loneliness.

The other maids were talking once
about me—I heard—
New girls think to keep themselves
all bright and unused
like the wallpaper behind the bed—
that doesn't last.

4

From the beginning the thought of Jim
went everywhere. A bird whistled
from a chink, a woman bent
to scrub the back stoop. With that,
the big sun at the land's edge
made as if to flip the whole thing
bloody over, the world
cloud by cloud passing to elsewhere,
dominion by dominion.

Stars picked out no tune.
The sea had just begun
to resettle its weight
and shadows dimmed on their tethers.

I imagined him, that we slept,
skiffs knocking together at quayside,
just beginning to dream
the voices of fishermen.

At Ringsend—the shadow of our joined hands,
the blurred swimmings of buildings
faraway, the milk light a glowworm breathes
to make a den of the dark.

I touched him for his pleasure, not mine,
so to avoid sin. I watched his face
when it had left itself, left behind
the whole keyhole city.

Love goes where miles go—the far surfaces.

5

On busy nights, I went down
past identical doors, muddied boots
standing as if waiting entrance,
to pour drinks. I stood ready
behind the bar, watched the men—
one in shirtsleeves, two bottles of Stout
hooked in his fingers, talked to a short man
with a head like a camel's.

The man down at the end
who came every day—his wife had died
the week before. I wondered did he still
let himself in softly, carry his shoes
up the stairs?

Jim. That you were
was true miracle, blue
your eyes, your eyes!
Good thing your luck
lit right in front of you.

At night, alone in bed
to think of him,
feel the hidden stars
turn faster and faster
like a skater wreathing her arms.

Then up with smoke, looking out—
I could ride the tops of the branches
with the slur of seafog
and huffs of coal
all the way to the topknots of waves—

That day I walked down Nassau Street
when it was loose to the breeze,
raised my head
in time to look at him—

Walking one late spring day
we heard a fiddle
flummoxed as a horse's sigh.
It seemed not to care
that it was roughly held
and the fiddler's hands seemed trying
to saw it in half from every angle.

He walked me down to a field
near the harbour's old skeletons
of ships, the empty distillery.

Among rusty springs
I knelt and unbuttoned his trousers.
The field disappeared taking its sour rust
and mulch, along with the stars.

6

I don't talk to his grave—
why speak to silence? I'd rather ask a stone
to tell him something—

He was like the halfmoon mare
I saw at the pony race—wouldn't let anything moving
pass her eye—it was win
or nothing.

Can the dead be at large
with the leaves
that shower the air with copper—
or would it be the lazy sleeving rain—

I told Jim I'd always hoped
for a family. We'd sit together
at table—cloth of lace covered by dish after dish,
Jim in the big chair.

If you're with me, you'll never have that,
Jim said. That rotten comfort

he wanted free of—even the language. So we lived
in different words, and I was Signora Joyce.
Some of the places
we stayed! Unfit to wash a rat in.

The children had nothing
to break loose of—only slack.
Georgio and Lucia.
Nothing attracts Georgio so much
as the cafe, sparks in a glass.
Lucia, locked up.
Free, she'd haunt the midnight cafes,
long to bare herself
in love. Ask a vulture the loan
of its ragged shawl.

At the last, the doctors sent me,
trusting, home to rest. You died
at 3 a.m., with no one.

Lonely your head and hands
in the grave fog, siftings on siftings.
Window to let in more dark.

Eire never unhanded you.
What is it
to be visible to strangers?

What is it to have the air,
untender and empty
rattle you, nudge to an edge—

In St. Stephen's Green:
treetops rushing the wind,
a scent of blooms floating ahead of itself,
a stillness far away
we could reach with effort.

A petal's sail unwrinkling,
light starring the crook of his arm.

❖NANCY

for Anne Chisholm, author of *Nancy Cunard: A Biography*

Peggy.
from
Jean.

NANCY CUNARD (1896-1963)

Nancy Cunard was born at Nevill Holt, a grand English country house, to Sir Bache Cunard (of the famous shipping line) and Maud (later Emerald) Burke of San Francisco. Nancy grew up to reject her mother's glittering social milieu—not only by joining bohemian Paris—but by writing hundreds of poems, running the Hours Press (one of the most successful small presses of the time, with the first solo Samuel Beckett publication to its credit), and making her love affairs open instead of covert. Nancy's loves included Surrealist poet Louis Aragon and—to the outrage of polite society—African-American jazz musician Henry Crowder. Her commitment to human rights led her to compile the immense and influential anthology, *Negro*, and to support (with money and courageous reporting) both the republican forces in Spain and the American Civil Rights movement. About *Negro*, Raymond Michelet has said that it was not at any time a reasoned enterprise. And neither was it a reasonable one . . . It was above all a work of passion, and impassioned. The same is true of Nancy.

1

The facts, please.
Without any hooly-gooly.

My mother was Maud (later
"Emerald.") My father, Sir Bache—*or*
my mother's great friend, George Moore.
When I asked GM he replied ambiguously,
"My dear, I'm afraid
I cannot say."

The manor's a boarding school now.
A glass-fronted box on the wall
in the servants' quarters still lists
our bells—mine says "Miss Nancy."
Is it too late
to order a romulo?

Too late—but I should listen to George,
who wrote on my copybook
when I was 13, "It is better
not to think that the moment
is always going by."

Life—after all—is beginning, as at the beginning
of all travel.

2

Cunard, Nancy?
First of all, she's not a Communist,
she's an Anarchist, perhaps. With so much injustice
who has time for ideology?

She loves peace,
Republican Spain, Blacks and Africa,
music, painting, poetry,
champagne. Hates fascists, snobs.
She's made some books: *Negro*, a big anthology.

Authors Take Sides, where British writers talk
about the Spanish Civil War. Many poems
and many poems unfinished.

Everyone asks me about the time
between wars. To hell with those days!
They weren't so super-magnificent!

I'd rather have a row of sparklers,
spraying fizzles. Or just a slab of light,
taste of apple, smell of sandalwood—
air sun light fruit beauty.

There *was,* now I think of it,
on a summer night, dancing, outside—
an accordion, violin, piano. Lanterns
in trees, leaves bright green,
veneered with light. Bob McAlmon yipping
like a mad cowboy, Kiki of Montparnasse
singing slowly of love and abandonment.

3

Some called me a fatal female—no,
just a Romantic, though hardly
harmless. Addicted
to the quick gift, I collected loves
without bothering to discard.

In this small way, I thought,
I can stay clear. But we're all caught
in what keeps us alive.

I was, finally, in this cobweb
of a body.

I married Sydney Fairbairn—the marriage a caesura
between good things past
and to come. My mother—

Her Ladyship—liked him.
They'd both lived in important places.

I loved one of Sydney's fellow officers,
Peter Adderley. We were together part of the summer
of 1918. In October Sydney wrote his mother,
"This last battle has been too long. . .
These damned Germans killed poor Peter,
at least he got badly hit and died
of his wound (stomach)." Broken,

I've always loved the sweet study
of fragments: some oddly curved root,
stick stripped of bark, its wood gleaming,
fierce sea-green flints, a shard
of pottery, a small blue
medicine bottle picked up
unseen, to look at
for the first time.

4: Henry Music

Henry: *Negro musicians comment running-fire on all women who come in. When this one appeared, so thin, so white, so fragile, we couldn't say it all. She came back night after night and always seemed to enjoy the music. One night as I was leaving I heard a female voice say, "Won't you sit down and have a drink?"*

Venice, the Lido strewn with society stars,
My cousin Edward and I had gone to the Hotel Luna
to dance, and there we saw people from another planet,
Afro-Americans, coloured musicians: Eddie South's
Alabamians, playing
out of this world.

That was the beginning.

30 years later I poured a libation
into the canal—for Henry—
what love we did make.

We transported a piano to Reanville,
and Henry became part of the Hours Press,
did circulars and parcels, laughing
at the strange hierarchy of English titles
as written for the Royal Mail.

He told me everything about his South,
till I knew why to be angry, why not to stop.
How come, White man, is the rest of the world
to be re-formed in your dreary
and decadent image?

For Her Ladyship it was as if a bomb
had exploded in her very house. Negroes
are not "received." They are not found
in the Royal Red Book. But if
he were an African prince, and rich—

As a little girl I dreamed of black Africa,
Africans dancing and drumming around me,
and I one of them, though still white.
Everything full of movement in these dreams;
it was that that allowed me to escape
in the end, going further, even further!
Apprehension sometimes turned
to joy, and even rapture.

After sex, Henry was almost gleeful,
exuberant as a boy. Swallowed
in Sir Bache's sable coat,
but unconsumed.

I wrote one blues for Henry to sing—
Back again between the odds and ends,
Back again between the odds and ends,
What once was gay's now sad,
What was unknown's now friends.

He went back to America, to his wife,
for the last time. Done.
It was a great strain
to be constantly exotic.
"Do find Henry in Washington," I asked a friend.
"You'll like him." A letter came:
"Henry Crowder's dead."

Then another letter, ending,
"Miss Cunard, I'll have you know
I was his one true and loving wife."

I sometimes thought he could make a song
out of the breeze clicking a latch
or some fine slippery stone I'd rescued.

Whatever else happened, Henry made me.
I owe him that. So be it.

5

24 Years Old
Dec., Jan., Feb. in the hospital in Paris

1st Op. Curettage
2nd Op. Hysterectomy
3rd Op. Appendicitis, Peritonitis, Gangrene with "a two percent
chance of survival"

I sometimes told a new lover
I'd deliberately had it out—
the freedom.

The world fixed coldly, afterwards—
deserved a mirthless smile. Emptiness
penetrated more—that is, I believed it.

Misfits mustn't reproduce: a law.
I outlawed myself from somewhere,
never clear where.

The blackest insult of insults: the woman
wants to surround a gigantic penis. O.K.,
I want it.

For Her Ladyship, madness was the most acceptable
explanation. In *Point Counter Point* Aldous Huxley
called me "The logical conclusion of money and leisure."

I was of course the woman
in *Eyeless in Gaza*, the episode when a dead dog falls
from an airplane onto two lovers
sunbathing on a sunny rooftop.

Being in bed with Huxley was like being crawled over
by slugs—interesting, but not addictive.

6

A knock on the door, a face: James Joyce.
Sullivan, the Irish tenor, was not getting
the acclaim he deserved. My mother's great friend,
Sir Thomas Beecham the orchestra leader,
could help. Would I use my influence?

Two weeks later he appeared again. Sullivan
must be engaged for grand opera. I explained
I'd talked to my mother, and she'd seemed
to hear. Now the matter must rest.

Joyce insisted—if I'd tried already
I would now try much harder. A piece of writing
might come my way, he hinted, for the Hours Press.

How pleasant he must have been
over a glass of wine, with friends.
I never saw it. One must read Joyce
with a great deal of strong drink.
Consider Anna Livia
accompanied by the flow of wine . . .

7

Each room I migrated to I arrayed
with my bracelets, strips
of African cloth, chiffon scarves in bright orange
from Woolworth's. Remnants of keeping
but not keeping.

My parents had no daughter.
What could I have done with one?

I still see myself standing on some doorstep,
holding the silver hunting dog
Sir Bache made, and willed me.

When I was a girl, we rode to the hunt
together. That didn't supply small talk
for the days I visited him, my sympathies
long since switched to foxes.

What I had from Sir Bache and the Lady
was sham. What they had—
eventuating in nothing.

Aragon, the most serious lover, the Surrealist,
wanted me to stay put,
set up house, behave. In Venice
he nearly killed himself—a punishment.
I never pretended to love him
every minute. Should I have?

8: Holloway (1960)

It unhinges one—being female with no career.
Careering. I was locked up for months
in a house almost as grand
as Mother's.

The patients kept looking around on the floor
for invisible things lost, whatever.

At night sometimes they'd bang the doors and walls
and then I'd bang too. I loved it.

Drink had nothing to do with my case,
but Fascism had. Damn Spain and all its doings.
I wish I'd seen it all in 1936, drunk
blood and bullets before being killed
the day Toledo fell. I was unfit
to outlive my cause.
Someone fixed on the moon.

9

I stayed on my own recognizance
(of a sort) in a hotel smelling of varnish—
above a pinball battlefield
detonating day and night—
technology's whizbangs
had definitely left me in the dust. I gave in,
went downstairs, persuaded a pinball youth
or two to join me in a glass of rough red.

One thing about wine—it suggests *more.*
A stumble breaks into a fall, as if the air
were equipped with chutes. I tried the short way down
one of those flights of stairs
which decorate the French Riviera. Stayed in bed,
cursing, then fell again, and stayed in bed
writing a poem, "Pain"—unfinished.

10

I meet my oxygen tent—caul, veil,
greenhouse to my shrunken violet.
Bed apart from the streets' miles
of stare, the sparse trees' concentration—
what's left of mine, to my poem—
propped on my thighs' parchment.
I don't remember my name, but can write.

It's dawn it's so late.

Inside, I'm a new woman, 23, 30?
From where this body?
I remember passages, stairs, pale blue,
the cold, known air.

The trouble with her, me—always thought of the end
before the beginning. Time, lost.

Is anything done?

JEAN

for David Plante

"The novelist Jean Rhys always liked James Joyce because at a party in Paris he tactfully told Nora to fasten the open zip of Jean's new black dress."
—Brenda Maddox, *Nora*

JEAN RHYS (1890 or 1894-1979)

Jean Rhys was born Ella Gwendolyn Rees Williams in Dominica, in the West Indies. At age sixteen she traveled to England with an aunt and attended Perse School in Cambridge, and after that the Royal Academy of Dramatic Art. She left the academy for the chorus of a touring company of *Our Miss Gibbs* and met her first love, Lancelot Hugh Smith. When after a year and a half their affair ended, she sat down to write their story: a diary after the fact. Some eight years later, in Paris, she was introduced to Ford Madox Ford. Ford suggested her new name, Jean Rhys, and launched her literary career. While Jean's husband, Jean Lenglet, was in prison, Jean and Ford became lovers (apparently with the encouragement of Stella Bowen, Ford's lover at the time). These experiences fed Jean's first novel, *Quartet*. By 1939 Jean had published five books, including *Good Morning, Midnight*. Then the war, along with numerous personal hardships (including the death of her second husband), erased her from the literary scene for nearly 20 years—until Selma Vaz Dias, an actress, placed an ad asking her whereabouts. Jean herself saw it, and answered. In 1957 Vaz Dias performed *Good Morning, Midnight* for BBC radio. *The Wide Sargasso Sea* appeared, to great acclaim, in 1966. Jean could finally live in comfort and have the beautiful clothes she'd always loved. To the end, she continued to write.

1: WORLD'S END

At age twenty, my first love affair ended.
I wanted to drink myself to death.

My girlfriend suggested a move: Chelsea,
a neighborhood called World's End.

A stationer's shop—
in the window, quill pens: red, blue, green, yellow.
I bought a dozen, and black exercise books, ruled,
and a bottle of ink, and an inkstand.
Some cheer for my new table.

After supper I pulled up a chair and wrote:
This is my diary.

This is one of the reasons
I believe in fate.

Only the books matter.
If I stop writing my life,
it will have been a failure.
I will not have earned death.
Only writing is important, only books
take you out of yourself.

2: ROOMS

Music here? If your room's quiet enough
you can hear it—
a high sound which is the nervous system,
a low sound which is the blood.

Trying to seem respectable, again
I give myself away.
The eyes widen a second, then narrow.
If it's a housekeeper, there's an excuse
not to come back. Landladies regret
they've engaged my room for another guest.

Then a higher room: more stairs, less light.
Dregs of a dozen cheap scents.

I saw a large room where people paid
to sleep heaped together. Others showed up,
spectators at the doss house.

A room's a refuge from the wolves outside.
From the nothing that steps forward
not the nothing that doesn't.

My favorite room didn't try to be anyone's.
It resembled a restaurant.

3: ENGLAND, 16

This wasn't England, this was never England.
The trains should have been red and blue
like the toy ones in Dominica.
I hadn't heard of tunnels.
After the first one I asked,
"Was that a train accident?"

Like always, I should have expected
something different. The awful zoo:
a lion who looked at me with sad eyes
and paced without stopping.
Hummingbirds flew confusedly
among hanging slices of bread.
The Dominican parrot was the most surly,
the most resentful bird
I'd ever seen.

Landing in Southampton,
I peered through a porthole and saw it all,
all that would happen to me.

4: LOVE

It's unlucky to say you're happy.
When you're happy, the street's a favor.
Sidewalks are pretty.
When you're not happy, you're the bottle
stopped with sand, the cigarette
stuck in the grate. Here because you're here
because you're here.

In this game without nets
everything slides off to zero.
A hen's egg. Love.

Once the worst thing has happened, who cares?

Love is terrible. You poison and stab
and shoot it and it keeps on gasping,
dragging itself through mud. Like Rasputin.

One does not get used
to feeling forsaken.

In the chorus we sang this:

We hear the serenade
To a pretty monkey maid
And now in jungle town
The moon shines down
Without a frown
I'll be true
to monkey doodle-doo.

I'm a bit of battered ivy
looking for an oak—an English Oak—
Won't you wait, Mister Fate?

5: LANCELOT

The name—like my whole life—
implausible, but true—

My first. The best was when
he held me, breathless, saying

"Little dear, little love."
I knew he was incapable of going away
and I was lost: "Anything, any way
you want." No past, no future,
blackness.

The nights—I'd meet him at a restaurant.
Then the sitting room
with its bright fire.
Then upstairs. The curtains closed,
a thousand years went
in an instant.

I got back to my cold room
near dawn, slept. Then I watched
for the messenger
who brought his letters.

What turned the light bitter?
A dream said, "It's the hill
all beings must pass." What hill?

It became part of me—sadness, I mean.
I didn't notice anything.

I thought—you're a useless person
and could never get a job
much less hold one.

First, my lover's cousin gave me money.
Then I lost even that touch—
a check arrived each Wednesday
from H.E. & W. Graves, Solicitors.
Graves, indeed.

After what was then called
the "illegal operation"—guilt?
Remorse?

Rest from hope, from despair.
Both are far away
along with your body.

Here you are. Where are you?

A bed to wake in. Coffee. Food.
A movie. A walk. Waiting to see where misery
will next take you.

It was a bright October and very cold.
The leaves looked like sailing birds.

Why do most people think truth's
a matter of placing a coin in a slot?
No coin. No slot.

6: MONEY

"Money thinks I'm dead,"
someone said.

The words "dry rot" make me laugh
like anything.

The waiter was uniformed,
but there was a louse on his collar.
Laughable—next they'll nest a tin of soup
on a garbage pail lid—Your dinner, Madame.

Once I went two weeks without eating
except for coffee and croissant in the morning.
One glass of wine sent me skyward.

Is everyone's repertoire so small?

Love, and smash-ups, and money trouble—
what fate means, a life
of the same syllables.

7: DOMINICA

When I say I write for love
I mean there are two places for me:
Paris (or what it was)
and Dominica, where I was a child.

Most lovely and melancholy place,
not very attractive to tourists.

Fires, hurricanes, riots—
typical Dominica.

Though Obeah is against the law
in the English islands, it's a gentle art.
"She magic with him" is Obeah for
He loves her.

The sound of the sea advances, retreats
like a door blown shut and open.

Mountain water against thin green leaf.

Diablotin mountain circled by its own birds.

I rode on horseback to the country place.
You rode along the sea, then turned left
into the land breeze
and the smell of green.

The gold ferns and the silver,
not tall like tree ferns but small and familiar.
Gold, green, and cool.

Mango trees, orchids
flowering out of reach, sun, heaven, hell
(possibly empty), sudden darkness,
huge stars.

Mother was there, but I stopped thinking about her.

"You had a little sister," she said,
"who died before you were born."

"Smile Please," said the photographer,
pulling the cloth over his head.
"Not quite so serious."
But my hand shot up, as if in warning.

The Black (the Catholic) cemetery
was lovely: candles flickering all day,
flowers (real and made of paper),
letters to the dead,
with stones for postage.

A jumby is a dead person
raised by the living. A living person
raised by the dead.

8: PARIS

Paris lifted you up.
Started everything over.

Montparnasse was the street that goes forever.
I'd point myself along it, a trace.
Part of first and next and last.

Streets made of water, nights, eyes.
Faint jazz, persistent as hope.

It was "America in Paris," "England
in Paris."

Long shining empty street.

I worked in Paris, but never long.
In my dreams and my jobs,
everything leads to a lavabo.

In Paris I met Ford Madox Ford
who helped me write,
who was (with Stella)
a horror.

The English press (I think the English
both naive and spiteful) reported that Ford
never cleaned his teeth. Hygiene
was not his problem.

The moon shines down
without a frown.

9

Money buys belonging.

Clothes are the best way—new ones
possible magic, possible happiness.
A dress does something for you
or it doesn't. So many beauties
I've sold, abandoned. My fur, which made me
lady. Fierce, fanged.

In Paris I made part of a living
adding my midnight blue gown (me in it)
to the crowd scenes of films.
I had to quit—too cold. The star's face
was blue under her makeup.

I tried selling the dress—no dice.
"No one would wear *this*
but a 'woman who makes night'."

I always wanted to be beautiful.
Long after it was too late
I slapped on makeup.

I open my lucky compact—my face
asking eagerly about my face.
The same answer.

10: HATS

The hairdresser bows. We've achieved
that most difficult feat: perfect ash blonde.
Combined with the right hat, anything could happen.

An old woman tries on hat after hat,
looking for the one to retrieve her
from plainness and age. Her expression
is terrible: hungry, despairing, hopeful.
The fat salesgirl smiles, a minor devil.

The girl who helps me is patient.
"The hats now are very difficult, difficult

to wear." "Tell me," I ask her,
"which one I ought to have."

I leave the shop with a hat. My hat.
Nobody stares at me, which I think is a good sign.

At one of our last meetings Ford wore a bowler:
a British burgher's hat. In prison,
my first husband appeared for visiting hour
with a piece of sacking on his head.

11: POSTURES

Everyone respects arrogance.
When you're a child, you're yourself.
After that, the postures
people force you to assume.

You teeter, unbalanced,
badly heeled, aching with the difference
between what you thought you were
and what you are.

Mishaps—
a laddered stocking.
Sadness trips up your heels.

I was at the bus stop saying good-bye
to a man who'd wanted (I refused)
to undress me, and—
my drawers fell off. Slowly,
I stepped out of them, folded them
into my purse.

It is very cold and gets dark early.
One meets dark figures in the road,
and frost and ice are everywhere.

A man following me looks into my lined face
and turns away, startled
at his mistake.

A little fame—and the neighbors
would like to arrest me

for impersonating a dead writer
called Jean Rhys.
They know me as no one—or worse.

Selma—who unearthed *Good Morning Midnight*—
said the kindest thing she'd heard about me
was that I'd died. She missed (thank God) the headline
of my latest trial: MRS. HAMER AGITATED.
ONLY HAD ALGERIAN WINE.

There have been months of fights—
starting with the wretch who killed my cats.
Ending with the magistrate.
He asked me did I have anything to say
so I said it.

Then the hospital wing of Holloway Prison.
Didn't mind the solitude. They clang the door on you
and shut the gossiping devils out.
I liked the people there—a Gypsy lady
who called cigarets "doggins" and London
"the smoke."

A minor triumph—the report said "Not Crazy."
Now I'm an old Hollowayian.
I know the songs there.

No one understands how easily
the words fly away and don't come back.
All the important things
reduced to ravings.

12

The fantastic is simply
what you didn't do. This goes
for everybody.

When our boy was born
he was already getting cold. William.
I had no milk. Soon he was dead
and required a tag for his wrist.

There's a song I translate
from patois—Because the flowers
are so pretty, they're dead in an instant.
One day and a thousand years
the same.

In between there are the little happy minutes.
Sensations—tree, a shaded light.
A plate of red apples on a table.

A moment
when I was walking along in the heat,
thinking then not thinking,
being intensely happy
for I existed no longer.
But still the trees and the soft wind
that smells of flowers
and the sea, and I was the wind
the trees the sea the warm earth,
and I left behind a prison a horrible dream
of prison. And my happiness—
impossible to write of it—active,
laughing with joy.

This happened walking along the road
from Théoule to Cannes
about two or three o'clock
one hot day in August.

How to write? I have no tools
and know only myself—worn down almost to roots,
a tree's old underpinings.

Only the books matter.

There is a lovely red flower
from the garden—pinky-red not to be believed—
so affectionate.